"This is the closest we come to Sinclair Ferguson's autobiography! The story of a time-travelling professor leading us to the pivotal event of human history! Another treasure to share with grandchildren."

Alistair Begg

Senior Pastor, Parkside Church, Chagrin Falls, Ohio

"Most stories begin at the beginning. But in this book, Sinclair Ferguson takes children back to before the 'In the beginning' of the Bible to put the love of God on display in the covenant between Father, Son, and Holy Spirit to call a people to himself. This book is imaginative, clear, and might just teach adults as much or more than it teaches children!"

Nancy Guthrie

Author of *What Every Child Should Know About Prayer*

"It sounds too good to be true. It really happened. God the Son came to earth to save His people from their sins. Dr. Ferguson takes us on a wonderful trip back to the moment that changed everything for you and me."

Chris Larson

President & CEO, Ligonier Ministries

"I really felt my heart burn within me as I read through this beautifully illustrated summary of the story I am in. I'm just off to read it with my five year old."

Rico Tice

Author, Founder of Christianity Explored Ministries and Senior Minister (Evangelism) at All Souls Church, Langham Place, London

The Magnificent

Time Machine

Sinclair B. Ferguson

CF4·K

10 9 8 7 6 5 4 3 2 1

© Copyright 2022 Sinclair B. Ferguson

ISBN: 978-1-5271-0791-5

Published by Christian Focus Publications,
Geanies House, Fearn, Tain, Ross-shire,
IV20 1TW, Scotland, U.K.

Illustrated by Martyn Smith
Cover and internal design by James Amour

Printed and bound by Imago in Turkey

The Bible version is the author's own paraphrase

This book belongs to:

Hi there!

Let's go on a journey in a magnificent time machine.

It can travel backwards through the centuries. I wonder where we will go? Now it would be scary to go on your own, so it's a good job this time machine can take passengers!

Get on board and come with me. Are you ready to travel in time — back to the very beginning?

Hey! Look at this! We're in the *1960s*. There's a spaceship going to the moon!

And now it's the *19th* century. I saw Queen Victoria.

That's an American soldier fighting for independence in 1776.

And there's Robert the Bruce at the Battle of Bannockburn in 1314.

Look over there—that city
is on fire! It's Rome!

The Sack of Rome took place in
410 AD. Now we've reached the
1st century.

Look out of the window.
Can you see the star?

That's Bethlehem.
It's the star God gave
when Jesus was born!

Hold on, we're going
even faster now!

Look in the rear-time
mirror: it's Daniel in
the lions' den!

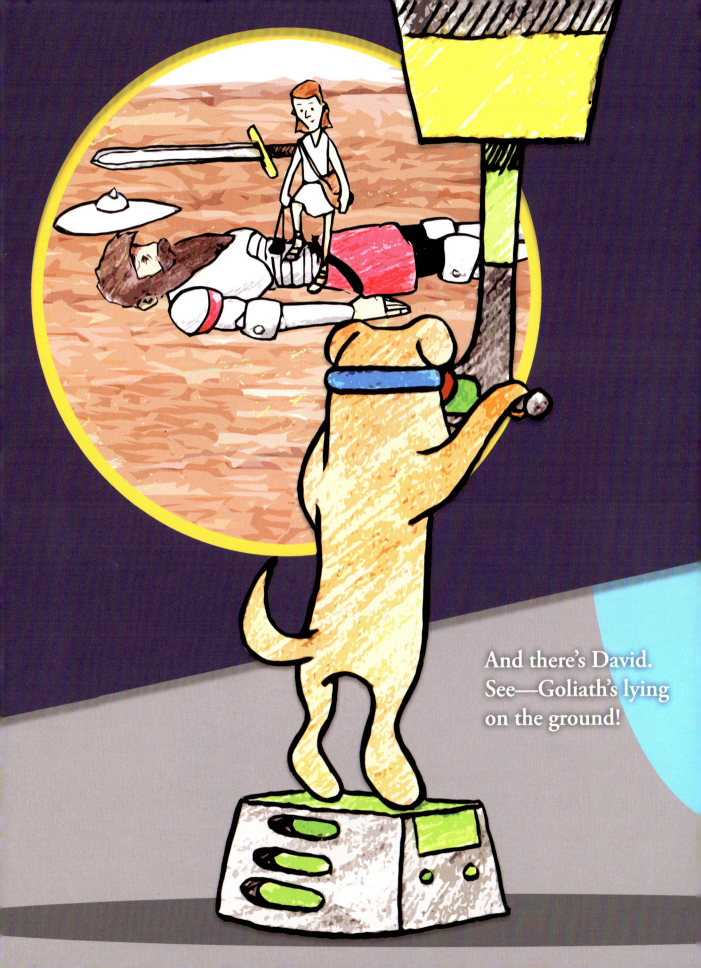

And there's David. See—Goliath's lying on the ground!

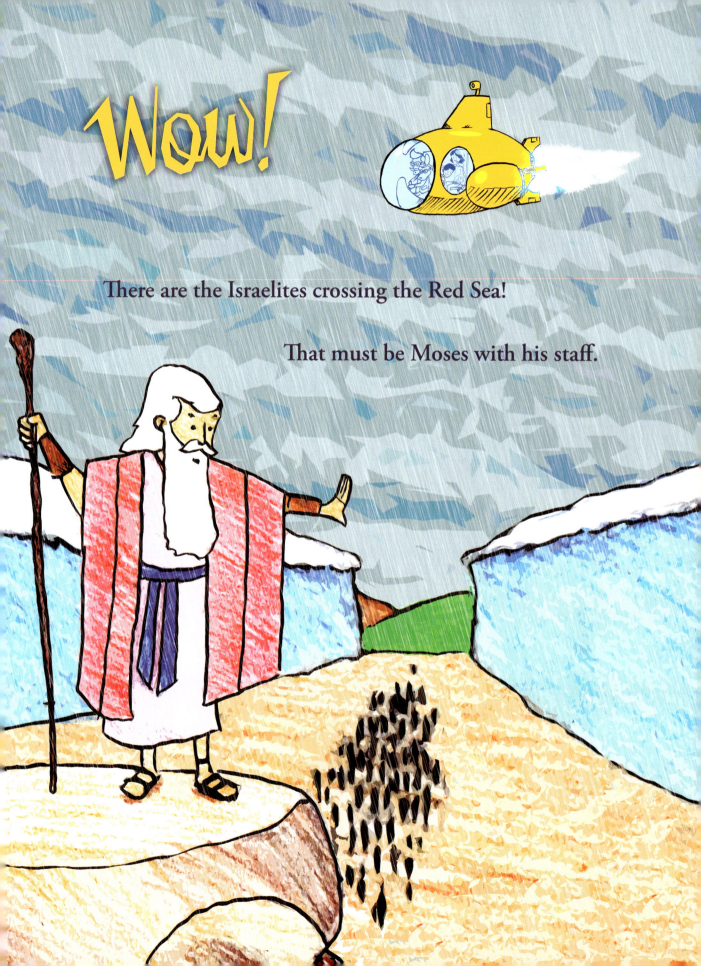

Now look at that man.

He has just walked past a road sign that says, 'Ur of the Chaldees'.

It's Abraham!

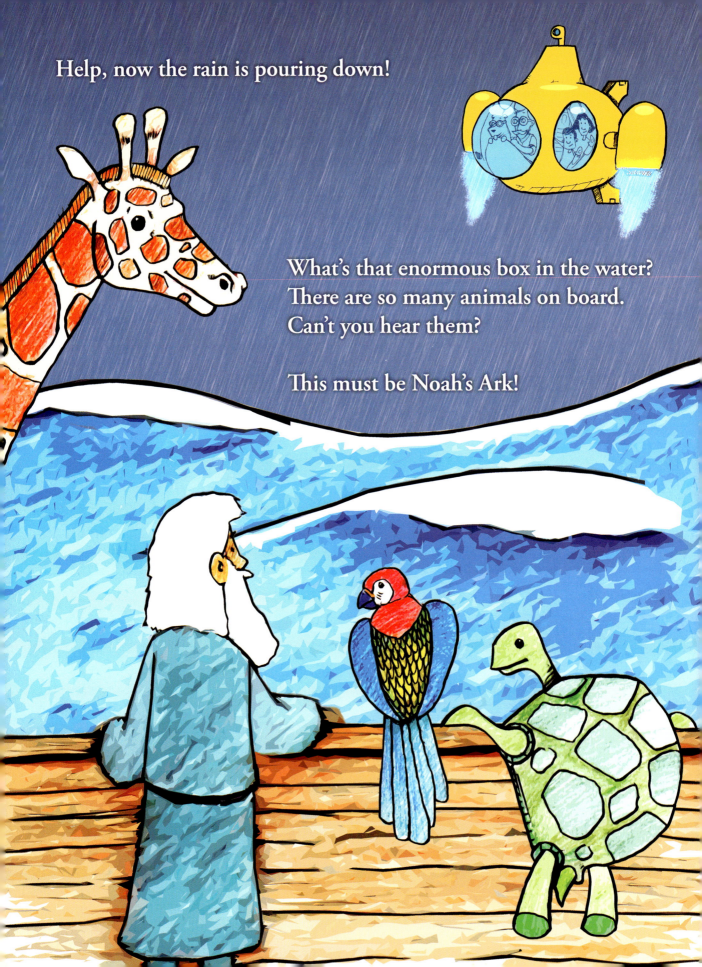

Help, now the rain is pouring down!

What's that enormous box in the water?
There are so many animals on board.
Can't you hear them?

This must be Noah's Ark!

This must be Adam and Eve. God is sending them away because of their sin.

They won't be able to live in the garden that God made for them. How terrible!

We haven't stopped yet though. We're still moving – but only just. We must be near the beginning of time.

What will happen next? Time travel is scary when you get near to the beginning.

Listen to that voice! Can you hear it? It is beautiful,
like music ... It is God the Father's voice.

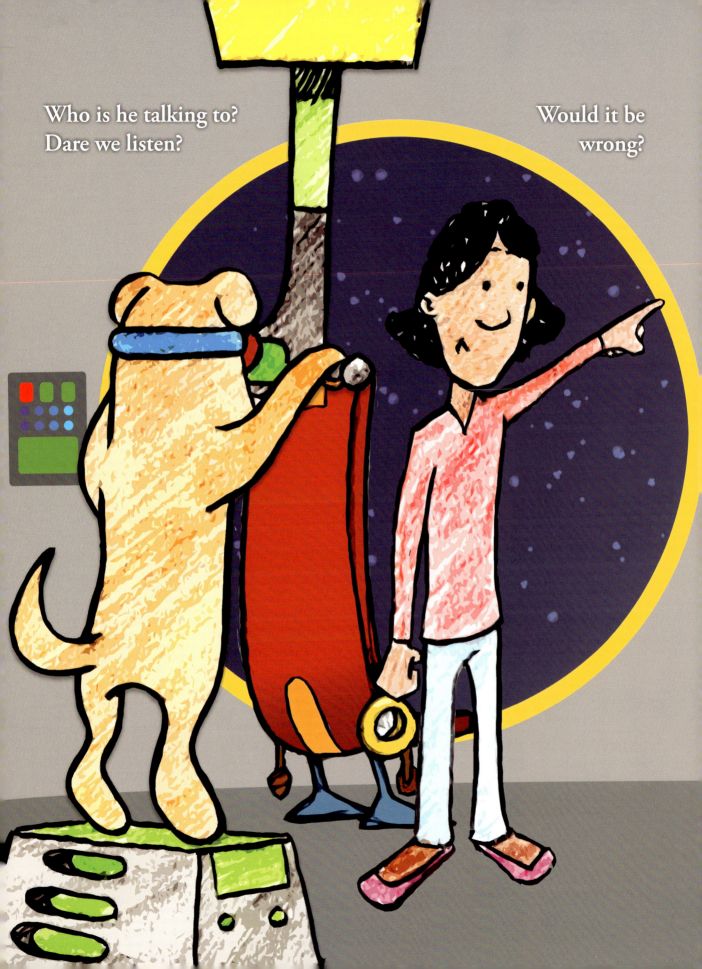

What is he saying?

'After Adam and Eve turn against us, we must save people from the terrible results of their sin. Here is the plan.'

Who's he speaking to?
Can you hear another voice?

'Father, I am willing to die in order to save men and women and boys and girls.'

That must be God the Son speaking!
But there is a third voice.

'We are agreed—I, God the Holy Spirit, will help people to understand what the Son will do, and how they can be saved from the terrible results of sin. The plan will work!'

What is this plan they are talking about? Did that plan succeed? Look at this! Pictures are appearing on the time screen. Perhaps this will show us what happened …

It looks as if we're going on another journey through time.

But it's forwards this time.

Noah has just come out of the ark, with the animals. God has promised not to flood the world again.

I've just spotted Abraham. He is looking up at the stars. God has just promised that the Saviour will come from his family.

Let's see what happens next.

There are the Egyptians trying to catch Moses and the Israelites – but they won't manage to.

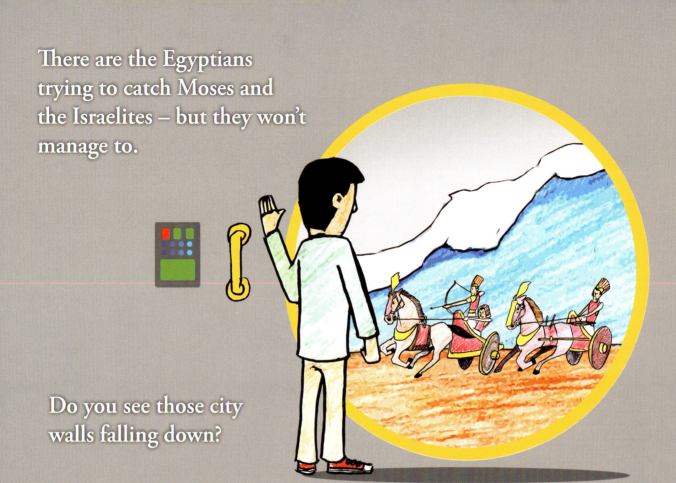

Do you see those city walls falling down?

It's Jericho. God has brought the Israelites to the land he promised them.

Look again! Why is that man dressed in special clothes? Why is he carrying animal blood into that small room in the temple? Let's listen in to the Father's explanation:

'We will show the people what you will do, my Son. Daily sacrifices will remind them of their sin. Once a year the High Priest will make a sacrifice, but you will be the Great Sacrifice! The other sacrifices are only pictures to show the people what you will do.'

There go Mary and Joseph on the road to Bethlehem—just
the two of them. See, over there—men riding camels! They
are looking up at a star in the night sky.

Listen to the Father again:

'A star will announce your birth. Those who have never heard about you will learn that you have come to be their Saviour.'

The Son says,

'I will go, Father.'

'They cannot be saved unless you die for them on the Cross. Are you willing to die for them?'

'Yes, Father, I am!'

'The plan will work.'

Now more pictures are appearing.

Jesus is baptised by John.

He teaches the people
and heals the sick.

He makes the lame walk
and the blind see! Look!

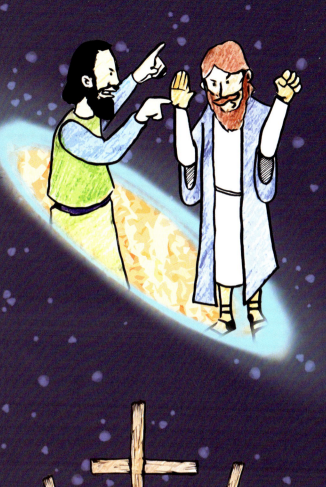

Why is Peter shouting?

I can see three crosses in the distance.

We're arriving in Jerusalem and that's the Garden of Gethsemane where Jesus was arrested.

Can you remember what happened next? Do you remember the crosses we saw in the distance ... that's where Jesus died.

But the cross is empty now.

Do you remember seeing Peter outside the empty tomb? That tomb we can see, is where Jesus was buried.

Jesus died for our sins and the Father raised him to new life!

There's Peter preaching in Jerusalem on the Day of Pentecost. The Holy Spirit has come and many people from all over the world have trusted in Jesus.

Now what's this on the screen?

It's a map of the world. Those arrows point to all the places where people have heard about God's plan.

And look, that arrow is pointing at your town and that's your street. There is an arrow pointing at your church. Hold on tight, we're slowing down. We're home!

I feel as if I have travelled for ever, don't you? What a wonderful adventure we've been on. We've got loads of stories to tell.

God's plan really did succeed!

Just in case you need a bit of help – here are some words that you can use to tell others about God's plan. They are from the Gospel according to John.

God so loved the world that he gave his only Son so that whoever believes in him should not die but have everlasting life.

John 3:16

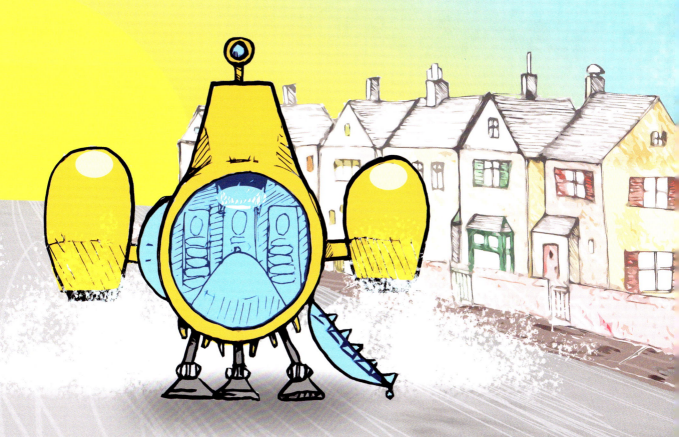

That is the plan.

That is the message Jesus wants you to tell others.

Will you?

More books by Sinclair B. Ferguson

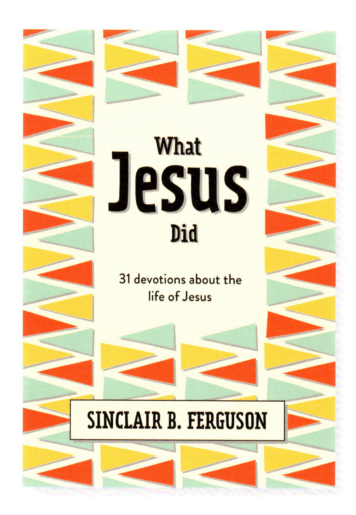

What Jesus Did
31 Devotions about the life of Jesus

Since before the beginning of time God has been at work. He created the world; he promised to send a saviour; and he sent his Son to die for us. With these 31 devotions and prayers you will see the impact of the life of Christ from before Creation to the Resurrection. Find out What Jesus Did through stories such as: Making Christmas Last; When Jesus Became a Refugee; and How Do I know Jesus Loves me?

You might also like...

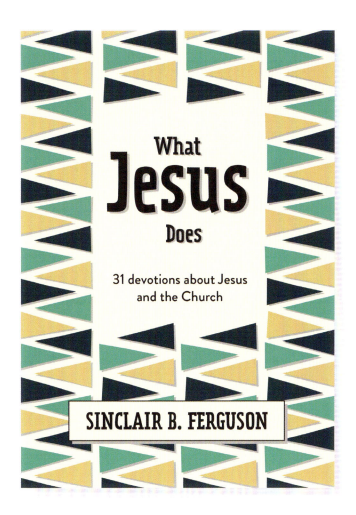

What Jesus Does
31 Devotions about Jesus and the Church

What is a life with Jesus like? How does the Son of God impact me? Through 31 devotions about Jesus, family and the church we discover what being friends with Jesus really means. Find out about Jesus, his friends and family, the disciples and the church through stories such as: Jesus Knows Your Name; Ready Steady Think; and Who Loves Church?